MAYA ANGELOU

L. PATRICIA KITE

In Consultation with Martha Cosgrove,
M.A. and Reading Specialist

LERNER PUBLICATIONS COMPANY/MINNEAPOLIS

This book is dedicated to my wonderful daughter, Sally Susannah Kite, who has always helped me work toward being a success in life. And with very special thanks to my friend, Jean Powell Ficklin, founder of our Afro-American Cultural and Historical Society.

Martha Cosgrove has a master's degree from the University of Minnesota in secondary education, with an emphasis on developmental and remedial reading. She is licensed in 7–12 English and language arts, developmental reading, and remedial reading. She has had several works published, and she gives numerous state and national presentations in her areas of expertise.

Lerner Publications Company
A division of Lerner Publishing Group
241 First Avenue North
Minneapolis, Minnesota 55401 U.S.A.

Website address: www.lernerbooks.com

Library of Congress Cataloging-in-Publication Data

Kite, L. Patricia.
    Maya Angelou / by L. Patricia Kite.
        p. cm. — (Just the facts biographies)
    Includes bibliographical references and index.
    ISBN-13: 978-0-8225-3426-6 (lib. bdg. : alk. paper)
    ISBN-10: 0-8225-3426-6 (lib. bdg. : alk. paper)
    1. Angelou, Maya—Juvenile literature. 2. Authors, American—20th century—Biography—Juvenile literature. 3. African American women civil rights workers—Biography—Juvenile literature. 4. Women entertainers—United States—Biography—Juvenile literature. 5. African American authors—Biography—Juvenile literature. I. Title. II. Series.
PS3551.N464Z744 2006
818'.5409—dc22   2005017033

Manufactured in the United States of America
1 2 3 4 5 6 – BP – 11 10 09 08 07 06

Contents

CHAPTER 1

GROWING UP

(Above)
President
Clinton
reaches out
to hug Maya
Angelou.
She had just
read her
poem at his
inauguration.

THE SKY WAS GRAY and gloomy outside Maya Angelou's big brick home in North Carolina. But the house was warm and cozy inside. Maya relaxed in a green velvet chair and talked to reporters. They were excited to talk to her and had many questions. Maya is a talented author and poet. She has written many best-selling books. Many of the books are about things that have happened in her own life.

In 1993, President-elect Bill Clinton asked Maya to read her poetry at his inauguration. An inauguration is a special ceremony for someone who has been elected president. It had been more than thirty years since a writer had been asked to read their poetry at an inauguration. In 1961, Robert Frost read poetry at President John F. Kennedy's inauguration.

The reporters asked Maya why Clinton had chosen her to read poetry. "He knows my work," she said. She also said he may have asked her because he realized she had a gift for bringing people together. Also, she believes that human beings are more alike than they are different. She believes poetry is strength for the spirit. It can inspire an entire country.

In preparation for the inauguration, Maya worked seven days a week. Many people visited, wrote, and called Maya to offer their ideas. People of all races wanted to be heard.

On January 20, 1993, Bill Clinton became the forty-second president of the United States. At least 250,000 people watched the ceremony, waving flags and cheering. Maya Angelou became the first African American woman to recite her poetry at a U.S. presidential inauguration. She called her poem "On the Pulse of Morning."

A ROCKY START

Maya Angelou was born Marguerite Annie Johnson in Saint Louis, Missouri, on April 4, 1928. Her mother, Vivian Baxter Johnson, had been a nurse. At this time, she was working as a card dealer. Maya's father, Bailey Johnson, was a hotel doorman. She had a brother, Bailey Jr. He was one year older than Maya.

That same year, the Johnson family moved to Long Beach, California. Once there, Bailey Jr. decided the name "Marguerite" was too hard to say. Instead, he called her Mya Sister. The nickname gradually became Maya.

In 1931, when Maya was three years old, her parents got a divorce. A year later, Bailey Sr. sent the two children to live with his mother, Annie

Henderson. She lived in the small town of Stamps, Arkansas. Maya and Bailey Jr. boarded the train alone. They wore tags on their wrists that said who they were and where they were going.

There weren't many jobs in Stamps. Most people didn't have a lot of money. In Stamps, African American and white residents lived in different areas of town. The railroad tracks and the Red River divided the two areas. African American

When Maya and her brother moved to Stamps, Arkansas, African Americans had to live in a separate part of town.

In the early 1930s, many African Americans worked on large cotton farms owned by white people.

residents lived in an area called the Quarters. Within the Quarters, most of the men earned a living by farming. The women worked on the farm and took in washing and ironing. Some African Americans worked on the large cotton plantations owned by white people. Others worked in the houses of white people.

MOMMA ANNIE

Maya and Bailey called their grandmother Momma. She stood six feet two inches tall. Her skin was the color of cinnamon. She was a big-boned woman with a wide face. She had high cheekbones and slanted eyes.

Twenty-eight years earlier, Momma Annie's husband, William Johnson, had left her. He took what little money they had. He left Momma and their two young sons, Bailey Sr. and Willie, in their one-room house in Stamps.

Annie needed to earn money. But she didn't want to go to work in a white person's home. And she didn't want to leave her boys in someone else's care. She could only read a bit and do a little math. The one skill she had was cooking tasty, stomach-filling meals.

Annie had a secret plan. One evening, she tested her strength. She carried heavy pails of stones on a 16-mile (25-kilometer) round trip to a local cotton factory and lumber mill. She wanted to

IT'S A FACT!

Laws kept African Americans apart from whites in Stamps and other parts of the South. Momma Annie taught Maya and Bailey that speaking to white people, even politely, was dangerous. Black children in the Quarters didn't see many white people in their daily lives.

know if she could carry heavy loads for long distances. Afterward, she knew she could do it. That night, she worked until early morning. She fried ham and boiled chickens. Then she made lots of meat pies. She carried the pies, along with an iron brazier—a pan for holding burning coals—to the cotton factory. When she arrived, she warmed the pies. There, a tempting smell filled the air. Annie sold delicious meat pies and cold lemonade to the workers for just five cents each. Soon she was selling meals to workers at the local lumber mill too.

For the next few years, Annie Henderson sold her meat pies at the work sites. Over time, she had regular customers. She built a food stand between the two work centers. Hungry customers came to her stand each day.

In time, Momma Annie's meat pie stand became the Wm. Johnson General Merchandise Store. Momma Annie was good to her customers. If Momma Annie didn't have an item in stock, she would order it. The Store was always referred to with a capital *S*. The African Americans of Stamps could buy what they needed. They could also meet and talk at the Store.

LIFE AT THE STORE

Momma Annie ran the Store with her son Willie. Willie was a big man who walked with a cane. He used the cane because he was paralyzed on his right side. Willie, Maya, Momma, and Bailey lived in the back rooms of the Store. The children spent much of their time in the front. The Store became Maya's favorite place. Every African American in Stamps visited the Store at one time or another. The children helped Momma ladle out flour, corn, sugar, and mash, or grain meal for customers. They put the purchases in thin paper sacks. When the weather was nice, the local barber set up shop outside the Store. He gave haircuts on the front porch.

THE DEPRESSION IN STAMPS

A huge economic downturn called the Great Depression (1929–1942) affected the whole United States. Many people lost their jobs. Others lost their homes and businesses. The depression hit small towns like Stamps especially hard. Families living on small farms could no longer afford food for their hogs and chickens. Over time, the U.S. government gave money, or welfare, to people in need. Maya's family was one of the few African American families in Stamps that was not on welfare. Food provided by welfare was the only thing that kept many people from starving to death.

In the evening, the children helped feed Momma's animals. They threw corn to the chickens. They mixed grain with leftover food and dishwater to make food for the pigs. Maya and Bailey often stayed to hear the pigs' contented grunting. Sometimes the children playfully grunted back. Maya enjoyed just about anything she did with Bailey. She thought he was the best person in the whole world. Maya also thought he was the most handsome. Bailey's skin was "velvet-black." His hair was curly. He was smart and funny.

From the window of the Store, Maya watched large wagons arrive to transport African Americans to the cotton farms of white people. Cotton picking was very hard work. In the morning, the workers were hopeful. If they picked enough cotton that day, they could buy food for their families and pay some bills.

In the evening, Maya saw the dusty, exhausted workers return home. They dragged their empty cotton sacks. The men's pay depended on the amount of cotton they picked. The more cotton weighed, the more they earned. But they often felt cheated by unfair cotton-weighing practices. Maya watched this scene day after day. She felt sorry for

A plantation owner's daughter weighs cotton to figure out the pickers' pay.

them. She formed a picture in her mind she would remember all her life.

Momma took good care of Maya and Bailey. She insisted that they keep clean. Every evening, even in winter, Momma made Maya and Bailey go to the well and wash. They did not have indoor plumbing. They scrubbed their faces, necks, arms, and legs. Then—except for Saturday nights—they had to do their schoolwork. On Saturday nights, they memorized their Sunday school lesson. Every evening, they said their prayers.

Momma kept busy running the Store and caring for the children. She made all of Maya's and Bailey's clothes. Momma used the same material for almost all of their clothing. Maya sometimes thought they looked like "walking wallpaper." The children wore shoes during the winter. But in the summer, Maya and Bailey went barefoot—except on Sundays.

SUNDAY IS SPECIAL

Every Sunday, Maya and her family attended the Christian Methodist Episcopal Church for African Americans. The church gave Momma a special title. She was an honored Mother of the Church. Uncle Willie was the head of the Sunday school. Before church, Momma made a special breakfast. She made eggs, fried potatoes and onions, yellow hominy, fried fish, and biscuits covered with sweet butter.

The church service was six hours long. During the church service, Maya and Bailey had to sit on hard wooden benches in the children's section. If Maya got bored during the long service, she thought about other things. She became very good at not hearing what she didn't want to hear. She also became skilled at listening carefully when she heard something she wanted to hear. Her favorite part of the service was the poetry of the gospel songs and spirituals.

Maya grew up in a religious community. Everyone, including children, spent several hours at church on Sundays.

AFRICAN AMERICANS AND TITLES

Whether at meals, church services, or at the Store, Momma was strict about manners. She told Maya and her brother that adults had to be given a respectful title, such as missus, mister, auntie, uncle, and sister. The use of titles to show respect dates back to slavery days. Slave owners gave each slave a name. Slaves could not change their names. Among themselves, however, slaves added respectful titles to their names, such as Missus Mary or Father George. The title system gave children an adult to turn to if they had a problem. If a child addressed an adult as John or Mary, the name suggested that the adult was equal to the child and not someone the child could turn to for help.

After church, the family ate a big dinner. The meal might include tomato preserves on buttered biscuits, fried corn cakes, pork sausage, green beans, and homegrown fruit. Maya loved the delicious, soul-warming food made by church women. One day, she thought, she would be a good cook too.

2 MANY CHANGES

AFTER ARRIVING IN STAMPS, Maya and Bailey never heard from or about their parents. Maya believed both were dead. She sometimes pictured her mother lying in a coffin, covered with a sheet, her black hair spread out on a small white pillow.

Then, at Christmas in 1934, Maya and Bailey received gifts from both parents. Father sent a photograph of himself. Mother sent Maya a tea set and a doll with blue eyes and blond hair painted on her head. Both Maya and Bailey went outside and cried after receiving the presents. If their parents were alive, the children wondered why they had been sent away. What terrible thing had they done?

A year later, a stranger drove up to the Store. He was a big, handsome man. He was Maya and Bailey's father. Bailey Sr. had come to take the children back to Saint Louis, Missouri, to live with their mother. Maya thought her father talked differently from the African American men in Stamps. He sounded just like a white man. She wondered if he was the only "brown-skinned white man" in the world.

As she and Bailey drove along in their father's gray DeSoto car, Maya began to cry. She wanted to return to Stamps. The children were afraid to meet the woman who was their mother. What if she laughed at them? (After dropping them off, their father returned to California.)

Both Maya and Bailey Jr. loved Mother right away. She was light-skinned and stood five feet four inches tall. She was the prettiest, most lively woman they had ever seen. Maya thought that she herself looked just the opposite of her birth mother. Maya described herself as being a "too big Negro girl, with nappy black hair," "broad feet," and a big space between her two front teeth.

At first, the children lived with Mother's mother, Grandmother Baxter. Grandmother Baxter had skin

as white as any white person. She spoke with a
German accent. She had been raised by a German
family in Illinois. Grandmother Baxter had gone to
Saint Louis to study nursing. While working at the
local hospital, she'd met her husband. Together they
had Maya's mother, Vivian, and four sons.

CITY LIFE

Saint Louis was quite different from the small
farming community of Stamps. Using her
imagination, Maya soon thought of Saint Louis as a
foreign country. It had many paved streets and

Saint Louis, Missouri, was already a big city in the 1930s.

large brick buildings. Coal dust from the city's factories filled the air. Buses, cars, and trucks constantly moved back and forth.

The African American schools in Saint Louis were different too. They were much larger than the white schools in Stamps. Maya and Bailey enrolled in Toussaint L'Ouverture Grammar School. They had been well trained by Momma and Uncle Willie in math and reading. They thought their schoolmates in Saint Louis weren't very smart. They also decided their teachers were snobs. They talked down to their students.

Life was much more interesting out of school. Grandmother Baxter

IT'S A FACT!

Toussaint L'Ouverture was a freed Caribbean slave who led a slave revolt in the late 1700s. Eventually, he became the leader of modern-day Haiti. He resisted European efforts to bring slavery back to Haiti.

worked as a neighborhood leader for the police department. The position gave her power within the community. She also had influence with the police department.

In late 1935, after spending six months at Grandmother Baxter's house, the children moved in with Mother. She was working part-time as a card dealer in a gambling parlor. Mother's boyfriend, an older man called Mr. Freeman, also lived with them. He was a foreman, or supervisor, in the Southern Pacific railway yards.

Mother's house was big and elegant. Maya and Bailey each had a room of their own. They had plenty of food. Their clothes were from a store, not handmade. They each had a radio. Mother gave them spending money to buy paperback books. Mother even gave Maya dancing lessons. When Mother entertained, she often asked Maya to dance for guests. This was a custom at the time. Any guest with a special talent—singing, dancing, or reciting poetry—might also be asked to entertain.

PAINFUL TIMES

Maya and Bailey were well behaved and did as they were told. But, still, they sensed that if they truly upset Mother, they would be sent back to Stamps. The fear of being asked to leave affected Maya and Bailey differently. Bailey began stuttering. Maya had terrible nightmares. Sometimes the nightmares got so bad that she was allowed to sleep with Mother and Mr. Freeman.

One of these times, Mother left the house early the next morning. When Maya awoke, Mr. Freeman molested her. Maya was very confused. She didn't know whether it was a bad thing that he touched the private parts of her body.

Afterward, Mr. Freeman asked Maya if she loved Bailey. "Yes," she said. Then he told her, "If you ever tell anybody what we did, I'll have to kill Bailey." Maya didn't understand what they had done or what there was to tell. But she wasn't going to let anybody kill Bailey. So she kept the secret from both her mother and brother. It was the first secret she had ever kept from Bailey.

Maya tried to forget what happened. She began reading more and more. She got her first library card. She especially loved stories like those written by Horatio Alger. In these stories, the poor main character always became rich. They became wealthy by hard work and honesty. Then the characters did lots of good deeds. Maya spent most Saturdays at the library. She was fairly happy at this point in her life.

LOVE OF WORDS

Maya had many favorite authors when she was young. She especially liked the work of the African American poets Paul Laurence Dunbar, Langston Hughes, and James Weldon Johnson. She also liked W. E. B. Du Bois. He was an economics professor and author of many books on the lives of black people.

Langston Hughes

W. E. B. Du Bois

But several months later, everything in her life changed. One day in 1936, Mother and Bailey were away from the house. Mr. Freeman grabbed eight-year-old Maya and raped her. He threatened to kill her if she screamed. Again, he said he would kill Bailey if she told anyone. Maya was terrified. She promised not to tell. But Mr. Freeman had seriously hurt Maya. She was in a lot of pain. Later in the afternoon, Maya went to bed. She hid her bloodstained panties under the mattress. Maya thought she had done something wrong. She thought that the pain was her punishment.

IT'S A FACT!

Maya had few places to go to get help against child abuse. That's not true anymore. The counselors at Childhelp USA are available every day. They can be contacted for free by phone at 1-800-422-4453. Their website is http://childhelpusa.org. It has a special section for kids and teens.

Later, Mother returned home and found Maya in bed. She thought that Maya was coming down with the measles. Mother told Bailey to get some cold towels to pat Maya's face. When Bailey left the room, Mr. Freeman came in. "If you tell . . . ," he warned.

In the morning, Mr. Freeman moved out. By then, Maya had a high fever. She sometimes called out to Bailey. She asked him if they could run away. Other times, she said she was dying or that she wanted to die. Her bedsheets were soaked with sweat. Mother wanted to put on clean sheets. But to change the bed, she had to move her daughter. Maya fought in terror whenever anyone touched her. Finally, Maya let Mother cradle her in her arms. Bailey began changing the sheets. As he did this, the blood-soaked panties fell from under the mattress. They landed at Mother's feet.

Mother rushed Maya to the hospital. There, Bailey insisted Maya tell him what had happened. He pointed out that the man might hurt another little girl. Again and again, Maya told Bailey that Mr. Freeman would kill him if she said anything. Finally, Bailey convinced her that this wasn't true. Maya told him all about the rape. Bailey started to cry. Maya cried too. Bailey then told Grandmother Baxter. Mr. Freeman was soon arrested.

AFRAID TO TELL THE TRUTH

Many people filled the courtroom on the day of Mr. Freeman's trial. Mr. Freeman's lawyer asked Maya many questions. The man asked Maya if Mr. Freeman had ever touched her body. Maya was afraid to say yes. She imagined that people would be angry with her. She felt bad that she had kept a secret from Bailey, which she had never done before. Everyone would get mad at her. So Maya lied. She said that Mr. Freeman had never touched her. She felt the lie was going to choke her right there on the witness stand. Maya had to be carried off the stand. She was so frightened that she couldn't walk.

Mr. Freeman was found guilty. He was sentenced to one year and one day in jail. But his lawyer got him out that same day. Several hours later, a police officer rang the doorbell of Grandmother Baxter's home. Maya was scared. She thought the police officer had come to get her. She figured he had found out about her lie in the courtroom. But the police officer came to the door for another reason. He told the family that Mr. Freeman had been killed—probably kicked to death. No one knew who killed Mr. Freeman. However, some people believed that Maya's uncles had taken revenge by killing the man.

Maya felt responsible for Mr. Freeman's death. She had lied in court. Maya thought her lying voice had killed Mr. Freeman. Right then, Maya decided to stop speaking. She thought that if she spoke, her evil voice might kill people. She stopped speaking so nobody else would die. The only person she would talk to was Bailey.

A GRAY FOG

Without speech, Maya learned to listen to everything. "I could just go into a room and I could just absorb sound . . . ," she recalled later. At first, her family thought her silence was because of the shock of being raped. But after a few weeks, her family thought she should be over the trauma of the rape. They thought she was being moody or sassy. Sometimes, Maya was spanked for not answering when spoken to.

By late 1936, Maya's family didn't know how to deal with her sadness and silence. So Maya and Bailey were placed on a train to Stamps, Arkansas. Once again, they were going to live with their grandmother, Momma Annie. Bailey cried. He wanted to stay in Saint Louis. But Maya wanted to leave. Not too long ago, she had feared being sent back to Stamps. Now she looked forward to once again living in the quiet, little town.

Maya did not speak in public for almost five years. Instead of talking, she turned her whole body into "an ear." She listened carefully to everything.

She remembered every word people said. Many people in the Quarters thought Maya was retarded. They talked about her as if she didn't understand what they were saying. But Momma Annie never gave up on Maya. She knew in her heart that one day Maya would speak again. For Maya, life passed by as if she were in a thick gray fog.

CHAPTER 3
FOR LOVE OF POETRY

IN 1938, when Maya was ten, she met Bertha
Flowers. Mrs. Flowers was the richest African
American woman in Stamps. Mrs. Flowers dressed
in fine, fancy clothes. She often shopped at the
Store. Each time, she noticed the silent little girl.
Usually, Bailey carried Mrs. Flowers's packages
home. But one afternoon, she asked that Maya do it.

Carrying the purchases, Maya followed Mrs.
Flowers home. As they walked, Mrs. Flowers
talked. She mentioned that she had heard Maya did
good written work at school. She also knew that
Maya liked to read at school and at home. But
Maya wouldn't speak in class.

Maya kept silent. Mrs. Flowers kept talking. Mrs. Flowers explained that no one could force Maya to talk. She pointed out how Maya loved the written word. She told her that the human voice gave special life to words in books. Mrs. Flowers told Maya that she was going to lend her some books. She said she wanted Maya to read the books aloud. Mrs. Flowers told her to say each sentence several different ways. She wanted Maya to understand that the way something is said can change a word's meaning.

Arriving at Mrs. Flowers's home, they sat down in the kitchen. Mrs. Flowers began reading aloud. Her voice was calm and beautiful. "It was the best of times and the worst of times . . . ," she said, holding a small book written by Charles Dickens. *A Tale of Two Cities* was already one of Maya's favorite books. But hearing it spoken was even more wonderful. It sounded just as lovely to Maya as her favorite church music. Maya felt happy for the first time in two years.

Mrs. Flowers gave Maya a book of poems. She told Maya that a person who truly loves poetry reads it aloud. She asked Maya to memorize one of the poems and recite it on her next visit. Slowly, Maya's voice started to come back.

BEAUTIFUL WORDS

A new world had suddenly opened up for Maya. She eventually read every book in her school's small library. She didn't understand all of the books. But she read them anyway. Maya liked how a story could affect her. She loved the power and magic of words. In between Maya's library visits, Mrs. Flowers brought her more books.

Maya never really thought about how books got written. It hadn't occurred to her that they were created by a person. Maya had a big imagination. She thought perhaps God and a writer got together and made a book. She saw the book coming out of a special body part that only writers had.

Eventually, Maya began writing poetry herself. After finishing a poem, Maya would go to a quiet corner of the Store. She'd read the poem aloud. She enjoyed the feel

IT'S A FACT!

Momma Annie loved to see Maya reading, especially poetry. She said poetry "will put starch in your backbone."

of the words. Customers in the Store sometimes complained. They said that Maya seemed to be always reading aloud and writing. Sometimes they had to knock loudly on the counter to get her attention when they needed help.

Momma and Uncle Willie encouraged Maya to read and write. Maya wrote regularly in a journal. Maya still wouldn't speak to people in public. Writing was a way for her to keep in touch with the world around her. At school, the other students gave oral reports. Instead, Maya improved her grades through better writing. She worked on her math with Uncle Willie at the Store. Uncle Willie helped Maya with her multiplication tables. He would tell her "do your sevensies, do your ninesies."

SEEING CHANGES

By the time she was eleven, Maya was doing regular chores. Each week, she received a ten-cent allowance. Maya gave the money to Bailey to buy her cowboy books to read. The family had fish fries. They went blackberry picking. Sometimes they held picnics. Maya played games such as hopscotch and jacks. Slowly she began to talk in public. At first, she only spoke to her family and a few special friends. But by 1940, when Maya was in eighth grade, she was talking as if she had never stopped. She was known as a bright and well-spoken child.

Maya also noticed the wider world around her. She saw the cotton pickers who came to the Store after work. The women's feet were swollen from being on their feet all day. The men's overalls and

Cotton pickers worked long hours for little pay.

shirts were torn from thorny cotton plants. Maya wondered how a loving and fair God could let all this happen.

Sometimes Maya and Bailey had to run errands for Momma in the white section of Stamps. White people were a mystery to African American children like Maya. Whites and African Americans lived very separate lives. Most African American children weren't even sure what white people looked like. A white-run hate group called the Ku Klux Klan (KKK) had done terrible things to African Americans in the area. The KKK sometimes injured or killed African Americans just because of their skin color. In turn, African American children learned to fear white people.

"LIFT EVERY VOICE AND SING"

In 1940, twelve-year-old Maya graduated with honors from the eighth grade at Lafayette Country Training School. Her all-African American school consisted of two buildings set on a dirt hill. In contrast, the white Central School had a lawn and a tennis court. Maya was at the head of her class. She hadn't missed one day of school. And she had never once been late.

THE KU KLUX KLAN

After the Civil War (1861–1865), white southern soldiers founded the Ku Klux Klan as a secret society. Its aim was to stop African Americans and other minority groups from voting or using their other civil rights to achieve equal treatment. Violence and terror were the tools Klan members used. They beat or murdered African Americans in many parts of the South. Klan members wore white hoods to hide themselves.

Members of the Ku Klux Klan try to scare a group of young people in 1938.

Only a few students in Maya's class would be going on to agricultural and mechanical schools. The training schools taught African American youth to be farmers, maids, handymen, carpenters, and baby nurses. But still, all the students had a future to look forward to. At graduation, all the children were dressed in their very best clothes. Maya proudly sat with her graduating class. She hoped the sunlit memory of that morning would never end.

Everybody sang the American national anthem. Then they recited the "Pledge of Allegiance." The principal gave a short welcoming speech. A Baptist minister led the crowd in prayer. Then the principal gave a longer, inspiring speech. He talked about Booker T. Washington, who had been born a slave in 1856. Washington went on to found and become head of Tuskegee Institute—a college in Alabama for African American students. He was a respected author. He wrote about race and education.

Next, a guest speaker spoke to the class. He was a local white politician running for reelection. He said that children graduating from the white Central School would go on to important careers. They would become famous scientists, inventors, and artists. The man then talked about how African American students might try to become sports heroes. He promised that if he won the reelection, he would see that Stamps would get "the only colored paved playing field in that part of Arkansas."

Maya was furious. Why did the students have to sit there quietly and be insulted? Was the man saying that African Americans could only succeed at sports? Why did they have to be judged by the color of their skin? A few moments earlier, the children had been proud and excited. After the man's speech, they hung their heads. They had once again been reminded that they should aim low in life. As Maya marched up to get her diploma, she felt angry and sad.

Next, Maya's classmate Henry Reed delivered a speech. Reed was the class valedictorian, or best student. His valedictory speech was called "To Be or Not to Be." It was based on a theme from Shakespeare's play *Hamlet.* Then Reed paused. Something was about to happen. Maya could just feel it.

Reed turned away from the audience and toward the graduates. Then he began singing "Lift Every Voice and Sing." Most African Americans thought of the song as their national anthem. James Weldon Johnson had written the words as a poem. J. Rosamond Johnson set the poem to music.

The poem talked about the rocky road that people sometimes have to travel in life. For many

James Weldon Johnson *(left)* **wrote "Lift Every Voice and Sing."**

African Americans, Johnson's poem was hopeful. While times were hard, eventually African Americans would get what they wanted and deserved in life. Soon everybody in the audience, including Maya, was singing along with Reed. Many people were crying when the singing stopped. Maya lifted up her head. Once again, she felt proud of who she was.

CHAPTER
4 LIFE IN CALIFORNIA

IN 1940, a few months after graduation, Maya had to move again. Momma told the children that they were going to California. They were going to live with their parents who were divorced. Mother had moved to Oakland, a town very close to San Francisco. Father lived in Los Angeles, far to the south. Maya suspected the change was to get her and Bailey

(Above) San Francisco, California, around the time Maya lived there

out of the South. California held more opportunities for African Americans than Arkansas did. An African American child there could become something other than a farmer or a cleaning woman.

At first, Maya and Bailey stayed in Los Angeles. Then they went to Oakland. They lived with Mother and Grandmother Baxter in a small apartment that was very close to the railroad tracks. The place shook every time a Southern Pacific train went by.

Mother soon married a businessman named Daddy Clidell. The family moved to a large boardinghouse in San Francisco's Fillmore District. A wide variety of people rented rooms in the house. Each room had its own special accent and personality.

The Fillmore neighborhood was alive with activity. Maya loved living in San Francisco. She considered herself part of the exciting city. For Maya and Bailey, San Francisco was beautiful. And it was freedom.

By 1941, when Maya turned thirteen, she had reached 5 feet 9 inches (1.8 meters) tall. She felt embarrassed about her height. She was taller than most of the people her age. And she was still growing. Sometimes the people in her boardinghouse asked her to reach for high-up things. Other times, they asked her to move heavy objects. She "felt like a horse."

At first, Maya attended a local high school for girls. But she was unhappy there. Her teachers had moved her ahead because of her good grades and her reading and math skills. But Maya had other problems at the school. The school had students from varied ethnic groups. Each group had its own prejudices. Some people judged Maya by her skin color. Other people judged her because she was from the South.

IT'S A FACT!

In the early 1940s, the Fillmore District of San Francisco was filled with people from many parts of the world. Japanese, Russian, Filipino, and African American businesses were everywhere. The people who owned the businesses gave the Fillmore District a thriving multicultural atmosphere.

A HELPFUL TEACHER

Maya's family moved her to George Washington High School in a white neighborhood. At first, she was one of three African American students there.

It's a Fact!

When Maya was a teenager and new in school, she was laughed at for speaking slowly. For a while, she'd fight whoever laughed at her. Bailey eventually told her to stop picking fights and just ignore people. The memory of those fights still embarrasses Angelou.

She felt nervous on the streetcar that she rode to and from school. African American passengers sat in a different part of the bus from white passengers. Maya felt uncomfortable, passing from the white section to the African American section. On the way home, she felt better when she saw black faces just like hers walking down the street.

Maya had always been a top student at her previous schools. But the students at her new school had strong educational backgrounds. These students spoke up quickly when a teacher asked a question. Unlike them, Maya felt she had to be completely sure of her facts before raising her hand. Sometimes Maya felt left out. But that was before she met Miss Kirwin, the civics and current events teacher. Miss Kirwin tried to bring out the best in each student.

She was always polite. She encouraged everybody, regardless of race or ethnic group. Miss Kirwin had a big effect on Maya. She helped open Maya's eyes to the idea of equal opportunities for all people.

New Experiences

In 1942, when Maya was fourteen, she received a scholarship to the California Labor School. The school was a college for adults. There, she studied drama and dance. At first, Maya was very shy in dance class. She thought her body was "cucumber-shaped," with knobs for knees, elbows, and breasts. Maya began performing for the Elks and Eastern Star service organizations. In her free time, she started writing songs.

Daddy Clidell liked to play cards. At home, he taught Maya games like poker and blackjack. He became the father that Maya felt she had never truly had. Daddy Clidell knew all kinds of people. He introduced her to African American street criminals, or con men. The men taught Maya how to avoid becoming a "mark," or target, for crooks.

When Maya was fifteen, Daddy Bailey invited her to spend the summer in Los Angeles, California. Bailey Sr. worked in the kitchen of a naval hospital. He was a member of two men's clubs, the Masons and the Elks. He was also the first African American deacon in the Lutheran Church. Daddy Bailey spoke fluent Spanish. He encouraged Maya to learn the language. Maya and her father even visited nearby Mexico together. Bailey Sr. had many friends there.

RUNAWAY

Maya did not get along with her father's girlfriend, Delores. The girlfriend did not like Maya either. When Delores called Maya's mother a whore, they got into a terrible argument. Afterward, Maya decided to run away. She packed sandwiches and put three dollars in her pocket. She spent the day wandering the streets of Los Angeles and reading in the library.

As night fell, Maya began searching for a safe place to spend the night. She found an old gray car in a junkyard and decided to sleep in it. As usual, she said her prayers before falling asleep.

In the morning, Maya had a big surprise. A ring of faces stared into the car windows. The faces belonged to homeless teens who lived in the junkyard. Maya explained she had no place to go. She stayed with the group for almost a month.

Finally, she telephoned Mother. She asked to come home. Mother was very happy to hear from her. She sent Maya a plane ticket. Soon Maya returned to San Francisco.

Back in San Francisco, Maya and Bailey began attending big-band dances. The dances were held in large public auditoriums, or dance halls. They danced the jitterbug, the Big Apple, and the Lindy Hop. The big band played the popular jazzy music of Duke Ellington, Count Basie, and Cab Calloway. Maya found she was a very good dancer. She picked up new steps easily. She even won a few dance contests.

But sixteen-year-old Bailey was changing. He liked to party and be wild. He and Mother fought about this. Finally, Mother told him to leave her home. As he packed, he gave Maya his precious books. She couldn't stop crying. Bailey was her best friend in the world.

IT'S A FACT!

The Lindy Hop came out of Harlem, an African American section of New York City. The dance was named after Charles "Lindy" Lindbergh. His plane had "hopped" across the Atlantic Ocean from New York to Paris in 1927.

LOOKING FOR CHANGE

Maya's life suddenly seemed empty. She had visited
Mexico. She had spent a month in a junkyard. And
Bailey had left home. Maya longed for a change in
her life. After much thought, she decided to get a
job as a streetcar conductor. The United States was
fighting in World War II (1939–1945) at this time.
Before the war, all the streetcar workers were male.
But with men away at war, women had taken over
many of their jobs. An ad in the *San Francisco
Chronicle* newspaper was looking for streetcar workers.

A San Francisco cable car in the 1940s

AFRICAN AMERICANS IN WORLD WAR II

More than one million African American soldiers joined the fight to end the racist leadership in Germany during World War II. They served in all parts of the military. But they still ran into the same unfair practices as they saw in civilian life. African American soldiers slept in separate barracks and ate in separate dining halls. Some African Americans became officers, but they still struggled to gain respect and authority.

One clear exception was the Tuskegee Airmen. They were trained to be pilots at Booker T. Washington's Tuskegee Institute in Tuskegee, Alabama. The airmen flew more than fifteen thousand missions over Europe between 1943 and 1945. Members of the group performed so well that they received more than 850 medals.

Seven members of the Tuskegee Airmen wave. This photo was taken in New York, New York, in July 1945.

Maya thought it would be splendid to be a streetcar conductor. She could wear a blue suit and go up and down the hilly San Francisco streets.

IT'S A FACT!

Some of the streetcars in San Francisco go up and down the city's steep hills. Underground cables (heavy metal ropes) pull and stop these streetcars, which are called cable cars.

She could wear a money changer on her conductor's leather belt. But Mother told Maya that African Americans were not hired to work on the streetcars. But Mother had also said that there was nothing Maya couldn't do if she really tried.

Maya returned to the Market Street Railway Company office many times. Each time, she was turned away with one excuse or another. But Maya didn't give up. She kept trying. One day, the receptionist handed her a job application to fill out. Maya was only fifteen. But she wrote on her application that she was nineteen. Maya wrote that her earlier job experience was as a companion and a driver. She had worked for a white lady, Mrs. Annie Henderson, in Stamps, Arkansas.

The railway company hired Maya. She became the first African American person to work on the San Francisco streetcars. By the time school started again, Maya's life had changed a great deal. She had her own bank account. She had new clothes that she had bought herself. Maya felt different. She had been a part of an entirely different world. Back at school, she didn't seem to fit in with the other students at school anymore. By 1944, Maya was bored with school. Sometimes she skipped classes. Many times she just walked around Golden Gate Park, a huge park in the city.

BECOMING A MOTHER

Maya decided she needed a boyfriend. She chose one of the handsomest young men in the neighborhood. She then boldly invited him to have sex with her. The young man was surprised but very willing. They borrowed a friend's room for a few minutes and had sex. Afterward, they went their separate ways. Maya didn't love the young man. Three weeks later, she found out she was pregnant.

Maya told Bailey first. He advised her not to tell their mother. Mother might make Maya quit high school before she got her diploma. Maya wore big, baggy clothes to hide her pregnancy. She pretended there was nothing unusual about her life. Mother was busy with business. She never noticed that Maya was pregnant.

In 1945, Maya graduated from high school. That same evening, she left a note on her stepfather's bed. She told her parents that she was expecting a baby. She was sorry. She didn't mean to shame or embarrass her family.

Mother wanted to know who the baby's father was. Maya told her. Did Maya want to marry this young man? No. Did he want to marry her? No. That was the end of the questioning. Three weeks later, Clyde Bailey Johnson was born.

ON HER OWN

When Clyde was very young, Maya decided to move. She wanted to show the world—and her parents—that she could take care of herself and her baby.

Maya applied for a job as a telephone operator with the telephone company. She was turned down for reasons that she thought were based on prejudice. She believed that she had been judged, again, by the color of her skin. Maya was told that she had failed a very basic test. The telephone company offered her a job clearing tables in its cafeteria. Maya took the job. She quit one week later.

Maya began looking for work again. One day, she passed a local Creole restaurant with a sign that said Cook Wanted. The pay was good. So Maya told the owner that she knew a great deal about cooking Creole style—a mixture of Spanish, French, and African cuisine. Maya also said she was nineteen, rather than seventeen. The owner saw no reason to question this since Maya was almost six feet tall and looked mature. She was also polite and respectful. The owner gave Maya the job. Maya asked one of Mother's tenants if he would please teach her to cook Creole. She learned quickly. She enjoyed creating recipes and cooking delicious food.

Maya rented a room for herself and Clyde in a large San Francisco mansion. She also fell in love with one of her customers. But he eventually left her to marry his old girlfriend. Maya became depressed. She had a dream of a kind, hard working husband. They would live together in a little rose-covered cottage. Maya longed to stay home and be a full-time mother. But none of this was happening. Maya began to think life would never get better.

RISKY BUSINESS

In 1946, eighteen-year-old Maya decided she needed a change. She traveled to Los Angeles. There, Maya found a babysitter for Clyde. She rented a room in the babysitter's home. Then she got a job serving drinks at the Hi Hat Club, a nightclub. Maya was good at remembering drink orders. She got good tips. Life began to look brighter. Maya's work shift began at 6:00 P.M. and ended at 2:00 A.M. Maya had time to spend with Clyde during the day. She liked to tell him stories and read him poetry.

After a few months, Maya met two female customers who often visited the nightclub. They invited her to their home for Sunday dinner. During the visit, the women told Maya that they were prostitutes—people who are paid to have sex. The women told Maya that their landlord wanted them to move because of their prostitution business. Maya pretended to be more grown-up and worldly than she was. She said she would rent the entire house in her name. The women could stay there, and Maya would help them find more clients. In exchange, Maya would take a part of the women's earnings. Maya was surprised when the women accepted the deal. At the age of eighteen, Maya was a madam—a woman who manages prostitutes. Maya never saw the customers. She just came by each evening to pick up her share of the money. Meanwhile, she continued her work at the nightclub. Maya soon had enough money to buy herself a new, pale green Chrysler car.

Maya was happy. She had plenty of money. Then, one day, Maya got into an argument with the two prostitutes who worked for her. They threatened to tell the police about her being their boss. Maya became terrified. What if the police took Clyde away from her? Maya went home and packed her bags. She abandoned her new car in the railroad's parking lot. She was afraid the police would trace her through the car. The next morning, she and Clyde boarded a train to see Momma in Stamps, Arkansas. There, Maya would feel safe.

BACK IN STAMPS

Maya arrived in Stamps in 1947. Momma and Uncle Willie seemed the same. But the war had changed Stamps. Many young people, both black and white, had left the town during the war. They had taken better-paying jobs in big cities like Detroit, Michigan; Chicago, Illinois; and New York, New York. When the war ended, few people returned to Stamps. But Maya discovered the Store hadn't changed. Shelves still held chewing tobacco and sardines. And Momma still had the wood-burning stove. As Clyde cuddled in Momma's arms, Maya began to adapt to life in Stamps.

Maya was a celebrity to the African Americans of Stamps. Just about everybody stopped by. They wanted to know all about the many wonders of San Francisco. People wanted to hear about a place where African Americans had opportunities. They wanted to learn about whites who were fair and kind.

After the War

World War II ended in 1945. Afterward, people found that job opportunities had changed. During the war, minorities and women of all races had learned new skills. After the war, some of these industries shut down. Other factories changed their machines to make different products. The white men returning from the war wanted their former jobs back. African Americans often found themselves unemployed again.

Maya could get used to the slow pace of Stamps. But she couldn't get used to racism. In California, Maya had lived mostly free of racist attitudes. And she saw no reason to accept racism in Stamps. She began to assert herself and live her life as she pleased. She began shopping in the white section of town. One day, Maya spoke back to a rude white salesclerk. Momma got the news quickly. She waited for Maya to return home. Momma had been warned that the Ku Klux Klan might come calling. Momma, Willie, and Maya would be in danger if Maya stayed. Maya had to leave.

(Above)
Maya looks
at a painting
of Clyde as a
young boy.

IN 1947, less than a year after moving to
Stamps, Maya returned to San Francisco. She
moved into Mother's big boardinghouse.
Maya's brother, Bailey, was also living there.
The walls were covered with Mother's
diplomas in cosmetology, barbering, and
welding. Mother had lots of energy. But Bailey
had less energy than ever. He used to be
happy and funny. He used to talk a lot. But he
had become quiet. He had lost the spark in his
dark eyes. Bailey had little time for Maya and

Clyde. He always seemed to be busy with something, but Maya couldn't figure out what that was. She worried about him. Many discouraged local young people got into trouble. She didn't want Bailey to get hooked on drugs.

Maya found a job as a cook at a small restaurant. She became friendly with the owner of a record store across the street. She began collecting blues and jazz records. She talked about her love of dancing. At the same time, Maya thought about her future plans. She wanted a good career. But there weren't many jobs for women. She thought about being a secretary. But she didn't have secretarial skills, such as shorthand and typing.

ENLISTED WOMAN

Posters in town encouraged young people to enlist, or join, the U.S. Army. Maya thought that if she signed up for two years and saved her pay, she could buy a house when she got out. She might even get professional training in the army. Afterward, she could get a good job. Mother agreed to find child care for Clyde.

Maya filled out the official army application forms. The army didn't accept women with children.

WOMEN IN THE ARMED FORCES

Throughout U.S. history, women have been involved in America's wars. Working as nurses, cooks, pilots, and spies, women have been a valuable part of the U.S. military. Recruitment, however, had largely ignored women until World War II. At that time, every available person was needed. The Women's Auxiliary Army Corps (WAAC) was formed, and it later became the Women's Army Corps (WAC). Women recruits took over support positions within the military to allow men to fight in the war. When Maya signed up, the war was over, but the military was still interested in keeping women recruits on the job.

So Maya checked the "no children" box on the application. She easily passed the Officer Candidate School intelligence test. She also passed the physical exam, despite her worry that the doctor would find out she had had a baby. Maya was accepted. She was told that she would leave for training in just a few months. Maya gave away most of her books. She donated her clothes to charity. She quit her job as a cook. She wanted to spend more time with Clyde before she left.

Then someone from the army recruitment center called. The person ordered Maya to come to the center right away. Maya hurried over. She assumed someone had found out about Clyde. But that wasn't the problem. An officer told Maya that records showed she had attended the California Labor School, where she had studied dance and drama. The U.S. Congress listed the school as a Communist organization. No Communists were allowed in the military. Maya had never been a member of the Communist Party. But she was quickly let go from the army for having attended the school.

COMMUNISM

The Soviet Union had a Communist government system. This system gave the government the power to set prices and own businesses. In the United States, individuals owned businesses. Prices were not set by the government. In the late 1940s and 1950s, the U.S. government became very worried about the spread of Communist ideas. The government didn't want Americans to favor Communism. People who joined the Communist Party or who went to Communist gatherings were suspected of being disloyal to the United States. The California Labor School came under this same suspicion.

PAID DANCER

Maya found herself without a job and with few clothes. Once again, she began thinking that she would never get anywhere in life. She took a job as a night-shift waitress in a small restaurant called the Chicken Shack. One day, a young man, R. L. Poole, rang the doorbell at Mother's house. He was looking for a female dancer to accompany his tap dancing act. The woman at the record shop had given him Maya's name and address, since Maya had frequently talked about dance. The army had punished her for studying at the California Labor School. But Poole might reward her efforts. Maya had also won dance contests in the past and knew current dances. She had never worked as a dancer. But Maya auditioned anyhow and got the job.

At her first public appearance, Maya wore a red, white, and blue costume that looked like a one-piece bathing suit. She carried a cane. Maya had never performed in front of an audience before. At first, she was so scared she could barely move. But after that, she enjoyed the applause.

Mother helped Maya make up new dance routines. Maya liked dancing. She hoped the situation would continue forever and keep getting better. But it didn't. One day, R. L. announced that he was teaming up once again with his former dance partner and girlfriend. Maya's job hunting began once again.

In the meantime, Bailey had fallen in love with and married a former classmate named Eunice. His new wife seemed to have straightened out his life.

A NEW RELATIONSHIP

One of Mother's friends needed a fry cook for her restaurant. The restaurant was in Stockton, California. Maya moved there with her son. She hired a baby-sitter called Big Mary. Maya continued to daydream about a good man who would love her and her son. They would live together forever in a pretty little house. She would have two children, a boy and a girl. She would not have to work but could stay home and cook.

In about 1948, Maya met an older man at the restaurant. The man, L. D. Tolbrook, was about twice her age. He appeared to be wealthy and attracted to Maya. They soon began dating. Then they became lovers. Sometimes, L.D. took Maya to visit various buildings. There, he would briefly chat with the women residents and then leave. Maya realized these women were prostitutes. But she also believed that L.D. truly loved and wanted to marry her. She had no idea he was already married.

L.D. was usually very sure of himself. But one evening, he looked quite tired and sad. He explained that he had lost a lot of money gambling. He told Maya that he couldn't pay the gambling debt. The other gamblers were dangerous criminals. They were going to come after him and hurt him. He would have to leave town quickly.

Maya didn't want him to go. She still hoped to marry him someday. Maya agreed to become a prostitute. She would give L.D. the money she earned so he could pay his gambling debts. After her first week at work, L.D. complained that she hadn't made enough money. He urged her to try harder.

One day in 1948, Maya received an emergency message from her family in San Francisco. Mother was in the hospital. Maya left Clyde with Big Mary. She then boarded a bus to San Francisco. Maya went to the hospital to visit her mother, who was recovering from surgery. She learned that Bailey's wife was also ill. Eunice had two serious lung diseases, tuberculosis and pneumonia. Maya and Bailey sat in the hospital waiting room and cried together. Mother recovered, but Eunice died. Afterward, Bailey was filled with grief. He quit his job. He acted strangely and looked unwell. When Maya tried to help him, he became angry.

During one of their arguments, Maya mentioned that she was working as a prostitute to help L.D. with his gambling debt. Bailey was silent at first. Then he got angry. He told Maya to get Clyde and return to San Francisco. If her boyfriend objected to this, Bailey said he would give the man more things to worry about than just gamblers.

CLYDE IS KIDNAPPED

Maya went back to Stockton. When she arrived at Big Mary's home, it was boarded up and silent. She asked a neighbor where Big Mary had gone. She learned that the babysitter had moved three days earlier. The other mothers who left their children with Mary knew of the move. They had picked up their children. Big Mary said that Clyde had been given to her. She would take him with her wherever she went.

Maya panicked. She hurried to L.D.'s house to see if he would help her find Clyde. His pretty wife answered the door. Maya finally realized L.D. was married. When L.D. came to the door, he became angry with Maya for bothering him while he was at home with his family. He told her he would visit her if and when he found the time. Maya suddenly realized how stupid she had been. She later wrote that "stupidity had led me into a trap where I had lost my baby."

After leaving L.D.'s house, Maya remembered that Big Mary had said something about having a brother in Bakersfield, California. The next day, Maya went to Bakersfield. She asked all over town about Big Mary's brother. Finally, she was directed to a farm on the outskirts of town. When she got there, she saw Clyde playing in the mud. Big Mary begged to keep the boy. But Maya refused. With Clyde in her arms, she fled back to San Francisco. They again moved in with her mother.

Important Decision

Once again, Maya began looking for work. Finally, she got a job planning menus for a restaurant in Oakland. The owner of the restaurant was also in the boxing business. Part of Maya's job involved driving fighters around before a match. This seemed quite exciting, until Maya actually watched a fight. She saw one of her fighter friends getting

hurt in the ring. Maya stood up and tried to stop
the fight. She was quickly fired.

Then one day, Maya met Troubadour Martin,
a man who had been a customer at the restaurant.
He offered her a job running a fitting room in her
home for women customers who bought clothes
from him. Maya guessed the clothes were probably
stolen. But at least the job would let her spend
more time at home with her son.

As the weeks passed, Maya began to think that
she was in love with Martin. But he didn't seem to
notice her attentions. His thoughts always seemed
to be somewhere else. One day, Martin said he had
something to show Maya. He drove her to a
horrible waterfront slum. Entering the building, she
saw addicts—people hooked on drugs—slumped
around the room. They all looked half asleep.

Martin wanted to discourage Maya from
having a crush on him. He made Maya watch as he
shot heroin into his arm. Maya thought it was one
of the scariest things she had ever seen. Right then,
she decided that the criminal life was not for her.
She decided that she was going to make something
special of her life. She just didn't know yet what
that would be.

6 SHOW BUSINESS LIFE

In the 1950s, Maya was a singer and dancer.

BY 1950, Maya was working at both a dress shop and a small real estate office. Her salary barely covered the cost of rent, food, and her five-year-old son's babysitter. Maya bought clothing at thrift shops. She usually chose something colorful. Maya loved color, headbands, and beads.

On days when she could find time, she went to Clyde's school just to watch him. After several visits, Clyde suggested that she not go to the school unless asked by a teacher. He also said that if she did visit, it would be nice if she wore sweater sets—a matching pullover sweater with a cardigan. Maya didn't understand this request at first. Finally, she realized Clyde wanted her to wear the matching sweater sets that the white mothers wore.

Maya sometimes visited the Melrose Record Shop. The store was in San Francisco's Fillmore District. The shop was a gathering place for local musicians and record collectors. The owner of the store was a very nice white woman named

IT'S A FACT!

Maya had lived in the Fillmore District in the early 1940s. But by the 1950s, it had become a different place. During World War II—when the United States was fighting against Japan—the U.S. government had forced Japanese residents into camps. They didn't come back. Russian residents moved to the suburbs of San Francisco. In the 1950s, the Fillmore was mostly an African American section of the city.

Louise Cox. At first, Maya didn't trust Louise.
White women were seldom that friendly to her.
One day, Louise offered Maya a job. Maya
hesitated. She wondered what the woman wanted in
return. But the salary that Cox offered was better
than what she was getting at the dress shop and the
real estate office. Maya decided to accept the job
offer and see what happened.

All kinds of people came to the Melrose
Record Shop. One day, Maya met a white sailor,
Tosh Angelos, who was of Greek origin. Tosh
became a regular customer. When he left the navy,
he began working in an electrical appliance store.
He and Maya enjoyed long talks. Tosh often told
Maya that he liked chatting with her because she
told the truth. They began dating regularly. Tosh
took a special interest in little Clyde.

MARRIED WOMAN

In 1952, Tosh proposed marriage to Maya. It was
the first time she had received a marriage proposal.
She accepted. Both Mother and Bailey gave a
hesitant approval. Maya Angelos quit her job at the
record store and became a full-time housewife. At
first, Maya seemed to have what she had hoped for.

But Tosh insisted that Maya stop seeing her friends. And he would not allow Clyde's friends to visit. They were not good enough, Tosh said. He even objected to Maya going to church. Maya didn't mind this behavior at first. She knew that Tosh liked being alone.

Church, however, had always been a big part of Maya's life. She missed going to church services. Eventually, she began going to church in secret. She went to a different church each time so Tosh wouldn't find out. Maya made sure not to become friendly with any of the other church members. But one day, she was so uplifted by a service at the Evening Star Baptist Church that she signed up to become a member. A church member telephoned her that same week. Tosh was furious. Maya kept silent and tried to adapt to her husband's way of thinking.

In 1953, Tosh said that he was tired of being married. Maya knew their marriage was far from perfect. But she hadn't expected it to end so suddenly. She had been faithful to Tosh. And she had let him have his way most of the time. For a while, Maya and Tosh continued living together to save money. Maya grew more and more miserable.

Then she needed some minor surgery. But due to complications, she had to stay in the hospital for several weeks. When she finally returned home, Maya told Tosh that she was going to Stamps, Arkansas. She wanted to visit her grandmother. She thought of Stamps as a safe and secure place—something she truly needed. But Tosh had bad news. He told Maya that her beloved grandmother had died while Maya was in the hospital.

THE PURPLE ONION

Maya and Tosh divorced, and Maya and Clyde moved back to her mother's house in San Francisco. Maya started job hunting again. She looked at many positions, but few jobs paid a good salary. Then she saw a sign: Female Dancers Wanted—Good Pay. The place was a strip joint. The women danced in fancy costumes. They were only partly clothed.

Using the name Rita, Maya auditioned and was hired. Maya wasn't expected to take off her clothes. But she was expected to sell watered-down drinks and expensive champagne to the customers between shows. It wasn't a good job. But Maya thought at least she was dancing. She ordered some fancy costumes and created her act.

Maya got along well with the customers. She even told them that they were buying watered-down drinks. The customers liked Maya's honesty. They often bought the champagne—which cost more—instead. The other women selling drinks noticed that Maya was making more money. They complained to the boss. Maya was given notice that her job was about to end.

One night in 1953, shortly before she was to leave, Maya saw three nicely dressed men and a lovely woman who had been sitting in the audience. She learned that the woman worked as a singer at the Purple Onion, a famous San Francisco nightclub. This unusual group began coming regularly to see Maya dance. One of the men mentioned that the female singer was leaving the Purple Onion. He asked if Maya could sing.

Maya had sung in church services while

IT'S A FACT!

The Purple Onion is a small nightclub in San Francisco's North Beach District. Famous comedians—such as Woody Allen and Phyllis Diller—performed there in the 1950s. Music groups, including the Smothers Brothers, got their start at the club.

growing up in Stamps. But she had never sung for money. Maya auditioned anyway, and she was hired. She decided she needed a stage name. Her first name, Maya, would be fine. But she needed a new last name. The Purple Onion bosses experimented with sounds. They changed Maya's last name—Angelos—to Angelou. By 1954, she had became Maya Angelou.

Maya's bosses at the Purple Onion taught her about being a professional, paid dancer. They gave her lessons on what to wear on stage. They also taught Maya how to act on stage. At first, she was afraid of appearing before a crowd. But once she started to sing, all her worries disappeared. Maya was popular right away. People told their friends about Maya's act. And more and more people came to see her perform. Maya was invited to be a guest on radio talk shows. She was asked to sing on television programs. Newspapers called for interviews. A small Maya Angelou fan club formed.

BROADWAY BOUND

One evening, friends told Maya that a Broadway musical had an opening for a singer. Maya wanted the job. She told her boss at the Purple Onion that she wanted to leave. But he said that she could not break her contract. Maya thought she had lost her one big opportunity in show business.

A short time later, Maya noticed people who looked familiar in the Purple Onion audience. Where did she know them from? Finally, she remembered. The people were performers in *Porgy and Bess*. The play was a popular folk opera—or musical—about life among African Americans in Charleston, South Carolina, in the 1920s. That evening, Maya received a big surprise. The actors invited her to join the chorus of *Porgy and Bess*.

The bright lights along Broadway in New York City in the 1950s included a sign for *Porgy and Bess*.

This time, with some help, Maya got out of her contract at the Purple Onion. The opera was being performed in theaters around the world. Maya had to leave Clyde once again. He would stay with her mother.

In 1954 and 1955, the cast of *Porgy and Bess* traveled to twenty-two countries. Maya was enjoying her new career until a letter arrived from Mother. Clyde was sick. He had a strange rash that doctors seemed unable to cure. Maya left the cast and returned home as quickly as she could. Clyde felt miserable and barely looked at her. Maya felt guilty. She promised that she would never leave him again.

THE STORY OF *PORGY AND BESS*

Porgy and Bess is an opera, or musical play, with four main African American characters. Porgy is a crippled man, who loves Bess. But Bess is the lover of Crown, whose job is to unload goods from ships docked in South Carolina. Sportin' Life, a dope seller, is the fourth character. Crown kills a man in a fight and leaves. Bess moves in with Porgy, who claims her as his own. Crown comes back for Bess, but Porgy fights and kills Crown to save Bess. Sportin' Life drifts in and out, trying all the while to win Bess for himself through tricks and cocaine. She follows him to New York. In the end, Porgy heads for New York to reclaim Bess.

GRATEFUL FOR THE GOOD THINGS

Maya was home, but life there had changed. Not only was she out of work, but Bailey was in prison for selling stolen goods. Maya felt empty and blue. She telephoned a psychiatrist and asked him to see her right away. At the last moment, however, she decided not to go. Could a middle-aged white man begin to understand her problems as an African American mother, an African American woman, and an African American artist? She didn't think so.

Instead, Maya visited a musician friend. This person insisted she make a list of all the good things in her life: her son, wonderful mother, excellent hearing, keen

IT'S A FACT!

Maya Angelou has had an amazing variety of jobs. As a teenager, she was a cable car operator, then a cook, waitress, and prostitute manager. In 1947–1948, she was again a cook and waitress, then branched into dancing, and went back to prostitution. In 1949, she drove boxers to their fights and fitted women with clothing. She worked in a record shop in 1950 and started singing in a nightclub in 1953. By 1955, she'd finished touring in a major American musical.

vision, and dancing success. Maya read the list she made. She saw that she should be grateful for all the good things in her life, not sad about the bad things.

Maya began taking theater jobs that allowed her to spend as much time as possible with her son. With his mother home, Clyde slowly recovered from his illness. Once again, he was his former lively self. For example, one day he walked into Maya's room to announce that he had changed his name. From that point on, his name was Guy. Why? No particular reason. It's just that "Clyde" sounded mushy to him, he said. And he was not going to change his mind about the matter. He didn't, and from that point forward, he was called Guy.

CHAPTER 7

LIFE IN AFRICA

IN THE 1950s, a group of young people formed a new popular culture in the United States. They were known as beatniks. The group was made up mostly of artists and musicians who didn't want to live a typical, ordinary life. By 1957, Maya had become a beatnik. She moved with Guy to a houseboat in Sausalito, California, across the bay from San Francisco.

Maya and Guy moved to Sausalito, California *(above)*, in 1957.

The houseboat was part of a commune. In a commune, a group of people live together, sharing chores and meals. For a while, Maya and Guy enjoyed this casual way of life. But in less than a year, group living lost its appeal.

In 1958, Maya and Guy moved to Laurel Canyon in Southern California. Most of the people living in the area were white. Maya tried to rent a house there. But she was told that it had already been taken. She then asked two white friends to try to rent the house for her. They did, and Maya moved in.

Guy faced racism at his school too. Maya didn't want racism to hurt her son's education. So Maya and Guy moved to the Westlake area of Los Angeles. People from many different backgrounds lived there. In Westlake, Mexican, Asian, African American, and white families lived side by side. Maya began to write while living there.

Meanwhile, a writer friend urged her to move to New York and join the Harlem Writers Guild. The group was based in Harlem, an African American neighborhood in New York City. The group was known for encouraging the work of talented African American writers, such as James Baldwin.

THE HARLEM WRITERS GUILD

In the 1950s, four African Americans created the Harlem Writers Guild. The four were John Killens, Rosa Guy, Walter Christmas, and John Henrik Clarke. They wanted to provide writing support for themselves and other published and unpublished African American writers. The goal was to preserve the experiences of African Americans using the written word.

African American writers were encouraged to attend workshops where their writing was critiqued. Discussions ranged from political events around the world to civil rights in New York. Some members included novelist Terry McMillan, and poets Audre Lorde and Maya Angelou. The guild continues to support African American writers through workshops and services available online.

In 1959, Maya moved to New York and made her first visit to the club. Her heart pounded as she read aloud to the group. She read her first serious piece of writing. Then she waited to hear what these talented writers thought of her work. When Maya finished reading, one member said her play was awful. Maya was hurt. She was ready to quit writing immediately. But another member told her not to be so sensitive. If she was going to be a writer, she would have to learn to accept criticism, or feedback, from other writers. If she couldn't do that, no one would give her helpful suggestions.

That advice made sense to Maya. She had been brought up knowing that to have talent was not enough. A person also had to work on improving that talent or skill. Talented or not, writing wasn't paying the rent. So Maya once again began to sing at nightclubs. Some of the clubs were nice. Other nightclubs were small and run-down.

FOLLOWING DR. KING

One day, Maya went to hear a speech by Dr. Martin Luther King Jr. He was speaking at a Harlem church in which there was standing room only. King had just been released from jail for his civil rights work.

Martin Luther King Jr. (left) was an important civil rights leader.

He was touring the country to raise money for the Southern Christian Leadership Conference (SCLC) programs. King was the SCLC's president. Its goal was to gain economic, civic, cultural, and religious rights through nonviolent action. People of all races and religions took part in the organization.

A GREAT LEADER

In 1955, Dr. Martin Luther King Jr. came on the scene as a civil rights leader. He was leading a protest against segregation on buses. His supporters boycotted, or refused to ride, segregated buses until the city allowed them to sit wherever they wished. The boycott was a success. But Dr. King wasn't finished fighting for the rights of African Americans.

Born in Atlanta, Georgia, in 1929, King studied to be a minister at Boston University, Harvard University, and the University of Pennsylvania. During his studies, he became a skilled leader and speaker. He was inspired by the teachings of India's Mohandas Gandhi, who believed in nonviolent protest and action. King carried these teachings with him. He practiced only peaceful forms of protest, such as sit-ins, boycotts, and marches.

In August of 1963, King organized the historic March on Washington. More than two hundred thousand people of all races took part in the march. The nonviolent protest demanded equal rights for all citizens. At the march, King delivered his well-known, "I have a dream" speech. The March on Washington brought worldwide attention to the racial problems in the United States. In 1964, King was awarded the Nobel Peace Prize. In 1968, King traveled to Memphis, Tennessee, in support of striking sanitation workers. On April 4, he was murdered as he stood on the balcony of his motel. His memory continues to inspire civil rights leaders all over the world.

Maya, along with the rest of the church audience, was deeply moved by King's speech. She wanted to help him and his cause. She began encouraging some of her show business friends to put on a show to raise money for the SCLC. The show, *Cabaret for Freedom*, was a huge success in 1960.

Not long afterward, Maya was invited to a meeting at the Harlem office of the SCLC. Three SCLC leaders whom Maya had met while organizing *Cabaret for Freedom* offered her the position of SCLC coordinator. Her job would be to coordinate, or put together, the organization's activities. At first, Maya was stunned by the job offer. She had never been offered such an important job. But there was no question what she wanted to do. She happily accepted the job.

Both adults and children, white as well as black, volunteered time at the office. The volunteers did whatever jobs needed to be done. Many white entertainers added their support to the civil rights struggle. Maya discovered that the world of racial prejudice in which she had grown up was slowly beginning to change. Maya sent out thousands of SCLC information letters and fund-raising invitations.

She enjoyed working for Dr. King's cause. The mood of the nation was one of hope and action.

MARRIED AGAIN

During this period, Maya met Vusumzi (Vus) Make. He was a representative of the Pan African Congress in South Africa. He was a lawyer and a member of the Xhosa tribe. Vusumzi was in exile. This meant he was barred from living in South Africa because he would not support the racist government there. At that time, South Africa was ruled by a white government. Most South Africans are black. Vusumzi was a South African freedom fighter. He was fighting for the freedom and rights of all South African people.

Maya loved Vusumzi's brilliant mind and his work for important

IT'S A FACT!

The Xhosa are one of the largest ethnic groups in South Africa. Nelson Mandela, the first black president of South Africa, is a member of this group.

causes. She also liked his charming accent. Vusumzi liked Maya too. Two weeks after they met in 1961, he proposed. Two weeks after that, they flew to London, England. There, they attended a conference of African freedom fighters.

In London, Maya met several women married to important black leaders and freedom fighters. After the conference, Maya flew back to New York City to find a new apartment. Vus flew to Egypt for more meetings. Maya found and redecorated the new apartment. She worked long and hard in her role as homemaker. She cleaned, ironed, and cooked fancy meals. She also continued to participate in the Harlem Writers Guild.

When Maya was offered a role in *The Blacks,* a play by French playwright Jean Genet, Vus refused to let her appear on stage. He felt it wasn't proper for the wife of an African leader to give a public performance. But after reading the play and talking with a friend,

IT'S A FACT!

Maya and several other female members of the Harlem Writers* Guild formed their own group. It was called the Cultural Association for Women of African Heritage (CAWAH). They raised money to help fight discrimination against women.

Maya *(center)* and the other actors in the play *The Blacks* wore masks during the performance.

he changed his mind. He insisted that Maya act in it because of the play's important message.

Vus worked long hours at the United Nations (an organization that works for world peace). Maya missed him. She was glad to have her theater role to distract her. But Maya also began to wonder if Vus was cheating on her. She found lipstick stains and the smell of perfume on Vus's clothing. Maya asked Vus if he was seeing other women. He said he wasn't.

Adding to these family problems, Maya began to receive terrifying phone threats from nameless callers. The callers told her that Vus was going to die or that he was dead. They said that Guy had been seriously injured and was in the hospital. Vus explained to Maya that all these threats came from the South African police. The police wanted to scare Maya and Vus, because he was an African leader and freedom fighter. Maya and Vus changed their home phone number over and over again.

Amid this turmoil, Maya and Vus received an eviction notice. Their landlord wanted them to move out of their apartment immediately. Maya hadn't realized that Vus, who was in charge of paying their bills, hadn't paid the rent on their apartment. Vus told her not to worry about the rent. They were moving to Egypt. Maya and Guy flew to San Francisco to visit Mother. Vus went to Cairo, Egypt, to make living arrangements for his family.

LIFE IN EGYPT

In 1961, Maya and Guy joined Vus in Cairo. The city was different from anything they had imagined. The air was filled with spicy scents. Street vendors of every kind offered their wares. Taxis competed for space with camels and limousines. Modern skyscrapers contrasted with the ancient custom of women dressed from head to toe in heavy, black clothing.

This street scene of Cairo shows Al-Azhar University. Founded more than one thousand years ago, the university is among the world's oldest places of learning.

In Cairo, Maya felt like a heroine in an exotic novel. Vus had filled their luxurious apartment with beautiful furniture, tapestries, and rugs. Maya met freedom fighters from all over Africa. She and Vus entertained frequently. Then Maya's maid informed her that the bills weren't being paid—not even the rent. Maya told Vus that she was going to get a job. Vus objected. He explained that proper women in Egypt didn't work. He assured her that they would eventually get the money they needed.

All the same, Maya got a job as an associate editor at a magazine called the *Arab Observer*. She was one of only two African Americans working in the news business in the Middle East. Through her new job, Maya met writers from all over the world. At first, she thought she would never learn enough about Africa's complicated affairs to be able to write intelligently about them. But she read every book, magazine, and essay available. She also consulted Vus. He was an expert on tribes, politics, leaders, and everything else in Africa. Maya worked at the magazine for more than a year. For extra money, Maya also wrote news for Radio Egypt.

NEW DIRECTIONS

Maya liked her work in Africa. But her marriage was unhappy. Maya still admired Vus's work. But she couldn't put up with his affairs any longer. Finally, in 1962, Maya announced she would be leaving for West Africa. Seventeen-year-old Guy enrolled at the University of Ghana, one of the best universities in Africa. Vus didn't try to stop Maya from leaving. He contacted friends of his in Accra, the capital of Ghana. Maya and Guy would have a place to stay when they arrived.

Accra was an amazing city. Maya wandered the open marketplace. There, black women sold everything from American face cream to fried ripe plantain chips called *killi wills*. Many black women dressed traditionally and walked gracefully with large baskets balanced on their heads. Others wore European-style clothes. Maya heard many languages, including Fanti, Ga, Twi, Akan, Ewe, Moshi-Dagomba, pidgin, and English.

Guy also got used to his new surroundings. One day, while out with some friends, he got in an auto accident and was seriously injured. Maya rushed to the hospital. She learned that Guy had a broken neck, arm, and leg, as well as internal injuries. After emergency surgery, he was placed in a full body cast. He had to remain in the hospital for a month.

Maya knew she needed a job to help make ends meet. She soon landed a job as a secretary at the University of Ghana. She was able to stay at the home of an instructor for free. The instructor was away on leave for six months.

After being released from the hospital, Guy needed care. He stayed with Maya for three months. Then, still wearing a neck brace, he moved into a university dormitory. Maya was going to be alone for the first time. As Guy brought his trunk to the door, he hugged her. "Maybe now," he said, "you'll have a chance to grow up."

Maya soon made new friends. They laughed, joked, discussed politics, and talked about how wonderful it was to be in Africa. She became so fluent in the Fanti language that she was once mistaken for a member of the tribe. As a gourmet cook, she enjoyed the local foods, such as lamb curry with side dishes of fresh pineapple, tomatoes, papaya, and mangoes.

Sometimes Maya daydreamed about how her ancestors might have been fishers or market traders in Africa. Her travels throughout Ghana eased her worries that American blacks had lost their African heritage after being sold into slavery. She discovered that many customs she had grown up with in Stamps, Arkansas, were similar to those in Ghana. These customs included calling people uncle, cousin, and brother as terms of respect and endearment.

By 1965, Maya realized that the United States was her true home. She had not come to Ghana to find her roots. But she found them anyway. Her people had survived, despite everything.

CHAPTER 8 THE WRITING PATH

In 1966, when Maya was thirty-eight, she returned to California. Two years later, she wrote and narrated a ten-part educational television series called *Blacks, Blues, Black*. The program highlighted African traditions still current in American life. Soon afterward her good friend, novelist James Baldwin, invited

(Above)
Maya came back from Africa with a new desire to write.

her to a small party. There, she met the wife of cartoonist Jules Feiffer. After talking with Maya, Mrs. Feiffer knew she'd met someone unique. She put Maya in touch with an editor at Random House, a large New York publishing company. The editor thought that Maya Angelou should write a book about her fascinating life. But Maya told him she wasn't interested in writing a book. The editor kept telephoning, and Maya kept saying no. Finally, the editor said he could understand her refusal. The job probably would be too hard for her, he said. Hearing that challenge, Maya immediately decided to write the book.

Maya's book was called *I Know Why the Caged Bird Sings*. It was published in 1970, when Maya was forty-two years old. It covers Maya's life from the time she arrived in Stamps, Arkansas, at the age of three until the birth of her son at the age of sixteen.

Maya received many honors and offers after the success of her first book. She was appointed Poet in Residence at the University of Kansas. She was also made a Yale University Fellow. Over the years, Maya would be given more honorary teaching positions and degrees by many universities.

MAYA'S FIRST BOOK

The title of Maya's first book, *I Know Why the Caged Bird Sings,* came from a poem. The poem is called "Sympathy," by Paul Laurence Dunbar. The poem explains that the caged bird still sings because it wants to be free. The book's dedication reads, "To my son, Guy Johnson, and all the strong black birds of promise who defy the odds and gods and sing their songs."

I Know Why the Caged Bird Sings was nominated for the National Book Award. Maya became the first African American woman to make the nonfiction best-seller lists. Her book became required reading at many high schools and universities. The book's theme shows that people can survive hard times and a harsh environment. They can live with courage, self-respect, and a love for life.

Columbia Pictures movie studio invited Maya to Hollywood to ask her to write a movie script for Alex Haley's book, *The Autobiography of Malcolm X.* Maya was enjoying her success. Only the death of her father affected her happiness.

In 1971, Maya's first volume of poetry, *Just Give Me a Cool Drink of Water 'fore I Diiie,* was published. The book was nominated for a Pulitzer Prize. Maya then lectured for the first time at Wake Forest University in North Carolina. There, she received the North Carolina Award for Literature. At the close of her lecture, Maya answered questions. The crowd of six hundred people was excited and enthusiastic. They stood up while asking question after question. It seemed Maya had ignited a spark. She had opened the students' minds to new thoughts and directions.

IT'S A FACT!

Maya was a good friend of both Martin Luther King Jr. and Malcolm X. She wrote about these friendships in her book *A Song Flung Up to Heaven*.

COMING FULL CIRCLE

In 1972, Maya met builder and writer-cartoonist Paul Du Feu at a party in London, England. Maya and Paul almost immediately fell in love. They were married at the Glide Community Church in San Francisco in 1973. Maya was forty-five.

Maya and Paul lived first in Los Angeles. Then they lived in Sonoma, north of San Francisco. There, Paul bought, rebuilt, and sold old houses. Maya spent a lot of her time at her longtime passion, cooking. She collected many cookbooks.

Maya also continued to write. In 1974, her poetry book, *Oh Pray My Wings Are Gonna Fit Me Well* was published. Maya's book *Gather Together in*

My Name came out the same year. The book took
her three years to write. Maya dedicated the book
to her "blood brother" Bailey. She also dedicated it
to a long list of "other real brothers," including
James Baldwin and Vusumzi Make. *Gather Together
in My Name* covers the time period in Maya's life
from World War II until Maya rescued her
kidnapped son.

Guy continued to bring happiness into her life.
Maya was thrilled when her grandson, Colin Ashanti
Murphy-Johnson, was born on February 2, 1976.

In 1976, Maya wrote two television specials on
African American life. She also completed her
book, *Singin' and Swingin' and Gettin' Merry Like
Christmas*. This book covered her life in San
Francisco from the time she worked in the record
shop and met her first husband, Tosh Angelos, until
the time she returned from the traveling tour in
Europe with the musical cast of *Porgy and Bess*.

Amid all her personal and professional
triumphs, Maya reluctantly decided to revisit
Stamps, Arkansas. The trip was part of a promise
made to two friends–correspondent Bill Moyers and
Willie Morris of *Harper's* magazine–years before.
All three had southern roots. "I was afraid to go to

Arkansas because of demons and I was afraid to
look creativity in the eye," she stated. It turned out
to be a very emotional trip. In Stamps, many
residents came to see her. They shared their
memories of the town, the Store, and Momma
Annie. She met people who had known Uncle
Willie and who remembered his patience. They
also remembered how he believed in teaching and
learning. Maya had come full circle.

Maya published a second book of poetry,
Still I Rise, in 1978. Her next book, *The Heart of
a Woman,* was dedicated to her grandson. This
book, from 1981, was a part of Maya's
continuing autobiographical series. The story
covers her life from the California commune to
her time in Ghana.

LISTENING TO HER HEART

As Maya grew more and more famous and
experienced, her marriage started to have problems.
She and Paul lived apart for a while. They decided
to divorce in 1981. Maya later said that she gave
each marriage her very best effort. But if the
marriage didn't work, she was brave enough to
leave. Paul decided to stay in the San Francisco area.

PERFECTING HER CRAFT

Maya is often asked how she writes a book. She explains that each book begins with a clear idea. The finished project, however, may turn out to be entirely different. When Maya is starting on a book, she writes in longhand on yellow pads. Once this is done, she organizes the material. She rewrites it over and over again. Sometimes she reads her work aloud to hear the rhythm of a piece. A finished autobiography may be hundreds of handwritten pages. When the project is done, she sends it to her editor.

Maya has stated that no form of writing is easy. Journalists sometimes call Maya a "natural writer." But that makes her angry. She works hard at finding just the right words to express her thoughts. She writes long hours to get control of language. Her goal is to make her readers weep or laugh. Sometimes it may take her two days or longer just to get one sentence right. "My responsibility as a writer is to be as good as I can be at my craft," she says.

Maya didn't want to see him every place she went. She moved to North Carolina, where she bought and expanded a beautiful home.

In 1982, Maya received a great honor. She was made a Reynolds Professor (a lifetime position) of American Studies at Wake Forest University in Winston-Salem, North Carolina. The Rare Books Room of the university library contains journals Maya wrote when she was about nine years old. The following year, when Maya was fifty-five, she published another book of poetry, *Shaker, Why Don't You Sing?* By then, Maya was receiving hundreds of fan letters per week. In 1986, Maya completed *All God's Children Need Traveling Shoes,* a book about her life in Ghana. *Now Sheba Sings the Song,* a poetry book, came out in 1987. *I Shall Not Be Moved,* another poetry success, was published in 1990.

By 1991, Maya was also helping to care for her mother, who had cancer. For a while, Mother was hooked up to an oxygen tank. Mother died in 1992 at the age of seventy-eight. That same year, Maya received the Horatio Alger Award, which was named after the author she had so loved to read when she was a child. Through the years, Maya had become like one of her early heroes—a poor person who, by hard work and honesty, lived to one day inspire others.

In January 1993, Maya recited "On the Pulse of Morning," the poem she had written for Bill Clinton's presidential inauguration. At the conclusion of her reading, the president hugged her, as the world watched on television. That same year, Maya celebrated her sixty-fifth birthday. Television talk show star Oprah Winfrey hosted a party attended by celebrities from all over the world. Winfrey, one of Maya's dearest friends, even designed Maya's dress for the occasion. Maya said, "Oprah is beautiful, tough, and bodacious, the kind of daughter I would have wanted to have." Maya's book *Wouldn't Take Nothing for My Journey Now*, published in 1993, is dedicated to Oprah. And 1994 brought the children's book, *My Painted House, My Friendly Chicken and Me*.

Maya had an exciting year in 1995. Her book, *The Complete Collected Poems of Maya Angelou,* was released. She also starred in the movie, *How to Make an American Quilt*. She played a character named Anna. In 1998, Oprah threw another party to mark Maya's seventieth birthday.

Maya received a National Medal of Arts in 2000. Two years later, she was awarded a lifetime membership in the National Women's Hall of Fame.

IT'S A FACT!

After appearing at the Clinton inauguration, many people asked for Maya's time. In 1993, her standard fee for an appearance was about $15,000. Her fee has grown to more than twice that much.

In 2002, Maya's book, *A Song Flung Up to Heaven*, made the *New York Times* Best-Seller List. She continues to write for children too. Maya launched a series in 2004 called *Maya's World*. Each of the books features a child from a different country–Angelina of Italy, Izak of Lapland, Mikale of Hawaii, Renee Marie of France, and Cedric of Jamaica.

Oprah Winfrey encouraged Maya to write a different kind of book. Oprah had eaten many times in Maya's kitchen. She wanted the world to experience Maya's wonderful recipes. Maya's cookbook, *Hallelujah! The Welcome Table,* arrived in

Maya prepares beef marinade in her home in North Carolina.

bookstores in 2004. "It's filled with wonderful stories and some of the best food you'll ever make," said Oprah.

Maya has had much success in her life. She has won countless awards. She has overcome huge struggles. But the one accomplishment she is most proud of is her son, writer Guy Johnson. "If I have a monument in the world, it is him. He's a knockout."

IT'S A FACT!

Maya doesn't normally use measuring cups and spoons. While creating the recipes for her cookbook, she hired a chef to come in and measure the ingredients she used in each dish.

LIGHTING A PATH

Maya continues to write. Her busy life includes lectures, television and movie appearances, and travel. Maya is "on" in public. She is witty and lively. But she is reported to be more serious and reserved at home. Maya has talked about the problems that come with being a celebrity. She knows that having reporters write about your works can give you a powerful feeling. But publicity brings danger too. Instead of being creative, a person begins to imitate his or her past work. Maya makes it a point not to be influenced by the media and what is written about her. She tries to stay centered. She listens to her heart. This way, her creative projects always stay fresh and new.

Maya, a great-grandmother, is often asked to speak at public events. She always lectures to packed audiences. Sometimes she dances on the lecture stage. Sometimes she acts out a problem and solution. Maya is noted for her many talents and

IT'S A FACT!

Maya has one grandson and two great-grandsons.

successes. She has said many times that she thinks of life as an ongoing adventure. Like her books about her life, her lectures always end with a hope-filled message.

In 2004, Maya gave a speech at Winston-Salem State University in North Carolina. Hundreds of new students gathered to hear her speak. Maya told the students that she believed DVDs and the Internet were dulling the minds of

Maya is often invited to be a speaker at public events. Here she speaks at the 2004 Democratic National Convention.

today's young people. She encouraged the students to read. "Learn as much as possible," she said. "Go to the library as frequently as possible." Maya also encouraged the students to be caring and giving to others. "Be a rainbow in someone else's cloudy sky," she said. "Light a path for someone else to follow."

GLOSSARY

civil rights: the personal freedoms guaranteed by law

commune: a small group of people who choose to live together and share expenses and chores

Creole style: a type of cooking that mixes Spanish, French, Caribbean, and African flavors and spices

National Women's Hall of Fame: created in 1969 in Seneca Falls, New York (the location of the first American women's rights convention), the hall honors U.S. women who have contributed greatly to U.S. society.

Pan American Congress: a movement toward commercial, social, economic, military, and political cooperation among the nations of North America, Central America, and South America

National Medal of Arts: the highest award given to persons who have supported or who have remarkable talent in the fine arts (painting, music, poetry, sculpture). The president of the United States makes the award.

racism: a false belief that one race is superior to another

segregation: the separation of one group of people from another based on race or ethnic background

Southern Christian Leadership Conference (SCLC): a U.S. civil rights organization started during the 1950s. The SCLC works to gain equal rights for African Americans and other minority groups through nonviolent civil protest and community organizing.

SOURCE NOTES

5 Gayle Pollard Terry, "Maya Angelou: Creating a Poem to Honor a Nation," *Los Angeles Times,* January 20, 1993.

6 Maya Angelou, *I Know Why the Caged Bird Sings* (New York: Bantam Books, 1993), 68.

12 Ibid., 22.

14 Jeffrey M. Elliot, ed., *Conversations with Maya Angelou* (Jackson: University Press of Mississippi, 1989), 4.

18 Angelou, *I know Why the Caged Bird Sings*, 58.

18 Ibid., 3.

22 Ibid., 72.

24 Ibid., 80.

27 Catherine Manegold, "A Wordsmith at Her Inaugural Anvil," *New York Times,* January 20, 1993.

27 Howard Chua-Eoan, "Moment of Creation," *People,* January 18, 1993, 62.

30 Charles Dickens, *A Tale of Two Cities* (New York: Signet Classics, 1997), 13.

31 Maya Angelou, *Even the Stars Look Lonesome* (New York: Random House, 1997), 130.

32 Maya Angelou, "The Distinguished Annie Clark Tanner Lecture," *Weber State University,* May 8, 1997, http:// departments. weber.edu/chfam/ FamiliesAlive/AngelouSpeech .html (October 14, 2005).

36 Angelou, *I Know Why the Caged Bird Sings*, 180.

37 Ibid., 181.

37 Ibid., 183.

41 Elliot, 4.

43 Angelou, *I Know Why the Caged Bird Sings*, 217.

64 Maya Angelou, *Gather Together in My Name* (New York: Bantam Books, 1993), 160.

76 Maya Angelou, *Singin' and Swingin' and Getting' Merry Like Christmas* (New York: Bantam Books, 1993), 238.

89 Maya Angelou, *The Heart of a Woman* (New York: Bantam Books, 1993), 271.

95–96 Jacqueline Trescott, "Maya Angelou's Pressure-Cooker Poem," *Washington Post,* January 16, 1993.

97 Elliot, 59.

97 Ibid., 149.

99 "Oprah Throws a Party," *Ebony,* June 1993, 118–120.

101 Natalie Houghton, "Welcome to Her 'Table': Maya Angelou Finds Poetry in Food." *U-Daily News,* November 2, 2004, http://u.dailynews.com/ Stories/0,1413,211~23528~ 2508416,00.html (October 14, 2005).

101 Teresa K. Weaver, "Maya Angelou's Final Chapter," *racematters.org,* May 5, 2002, http://www.racematters.org/ mayaangeloufinalchapter.htm (October 14, 2005).

103 Kevin T. Walker, "Angelou to Freshmen: Be Your Best." *New York Amsterdam News,* September 2, 2004, 36.

103 Ibid.

SELECTED BIBLIOGRAPHY

Angelou, Maya. *All God's Children Need Traveling Shoes.* New York: Vintage Books, 1991.

Angelou, Maya. *The Complete Collected Poems of Maya Angelou.* New York: Random House, 1994.

Angelou, Maya. *Even the Stars Look Lonesome.* New York: Random House, 1997.

Angelou, Maya. *Gather Together in My Name.* New York: Bantam Books, 1993.

Angelou, Maya. *The Heart of a Woman.* New York: Bantam, 1993.

Angelou, Maya. *I Know Why the Caged Bird Sings.* New York: Bantam Books, 1993.

Angelou, Maya. *Singin' and Swingin' and Getting Merry Like Christmas.* New York: Bantam Books, 1993.

Angelou, Maya. *Wouldn't Take Nothing for My Journey Now.* New York: Bantam Books, 1994.

Bloom, Harold, ed. *Black American Women Fiction Writers.* New York: Chelsea House Publishers, 1995.

Bredeson, Carmen. *American Writers of the 20th Century.* Berkeley Heights, NJ: Enslow Publishers, 1996.

Brown, Ray B., ed. *Contemporary Heroes and Heroines.* New York: Gale Research, 1990.

Chua-Eoan, Howard. "Moment of Creation." *People,* January 18, 1993, 62.

"Education." *Jet,* July 11, 1994, 20.

Elliot, Jeffrey M., ed. *Conversations with Maya Angelou.* Jackson: University Press of Mississippi, 1989.

Graham, Judith, ed. *Current Biography Yearbook.* New York: H. W. Wilson, 1994.

Hagen, Lyman B. *Heart of a Woman, Mind of a Writer, and Soul of a Poet.* New York: University Press of America, 1997.

Haughton, Natalie. "Welcome to Her 'Table': Maya Angelou Finds Poetry in Food." *U-Daily News.* November 2, 2004, http://u.dailynews.com/cda/article (October 15, 2005).

International Who's Who. London: Europa Publications, 1993–1994.

Jennings, Peter, and David Brinkley. Clinton Inauguration. VHS. ABC News, 1993.

Kranz, Rachel. *Black Americans.* New York: Facts on File, 1992.

Lambert, Paul. "Chapter and Verse." *People,* October 3, 1994, 108–110.

Manegold, Catherine. "A Wordsmith at Her Inaugural Anvil." *New York Times,* January 20, 1993.

"Martin Luther King, Jr." *Encylopaedia Brittanica's Guide to Black History.* http://search.eb.com/Blackhistory/article. (May 28, 2005).

"Martin Luther King, Jr." *MSN Encarta Premium.* http://encarta.msn.com/encyclopedia_761557424/King_Martin_Luther_Jr.html, (May 28, 2005).

Meroney, John. "The Real Maya Angelou." *American Spectator,* March 1993, 68.

Moritz, Charles, ed. *Current Biography.* New York: H. W. Wilson, 1974.

New Lincoln Library Encyclopedia. Vol. 3. Columbus, OH: Frontier Press Company, 1981.

"Oprah Throws a Party." *Ebony,* June 1993, 118–120.

Rosen, Sage. "Poet, Author Angelou to Visit Lawlor." *Nevada Sagebrush,* May 3, 2005.

Smith, Jessie Carney, ed. *Notable Black American Women.* Detroit: Gale Research, 1992.

Smith, Sande, ed. *Who's Who in African-American History.* New York: Smithmark, 1994.

Spradling, Mary Mace, ed. *In Black and White.* Detroit: Gale Research, 1980.

Terry, Gayle Pollard. "Maya Angelou, Creating a Poem to Honor a Nation." *Los Angeles Times,* January 20, 1993.

"This Week in Black History," *Jet,* May 13, 1995, 20.

Trescott, Jacqueline. "Maya Angelou's Pressure-Cooker Poem." *Washington Post,* January 16, 1993.

Urdang, Laurence, ed. *The Time Tables of American History.* New York: Simon & Schuster, 1981.

Walker, T. Kevin. "Angelou to Freshmen: Be Your Best." *New York Amsterdam News,* September 2, 2004, 36.

Weaver, Teresa K. "Maya Angelou's Final Chapter," *racematters.org.* May 5, 2002, http://www.racematters.org/mayaangeloufinalchapter.htm. (October 14, 2005).

FURTHER READING AND WEBSITES

Benson, Michael. *Malcolm X.* Minneapolis: Lerner Publications Company, 2005.

Carrick Hill, Laban. *Harlem Stomp! A Cultural History of the Harlem Renaissance.* New York: Megan Tingley Books, 2004.

Darby, Jean. *Martin Luther King Jr.* Minneapolis: Lerner Publications Company, 2005.

Di Piazza, Domenica. *Arkansas.* Minneapolis: Lerner Publications Company, 2002.

Finlayson, Reggie. *We Shall Overcome: The History of the American Civil Rights Movement.* Minneapolis: Lerner Publications Company, 2003.

Haskins, Jim, et al. *Black Stars of the Harlem Renaissance.* Hoboken, NJ: Jossey-Bass, 2002.

The King Center
http://www.thekingcenter.org
Founded by Coretta Scott King, the King Center in Atlanta, Georgia, is the official living memorial to Dr. King and his work. It includes recordings from King's speeches as well as biographical information on Martin Luther King Jr. and Coretta Scott King, and much more.

Krohn, Katherine. *Oprah Winfrey.* Minneapolis: Lerner Publications Company, 2005.

Maya Angelou--The Official Website
http://www.mayaangelou.com/
The official website of Maya Angelou provides biographical information as well as links to products such as books and also the Maya Angelou Hallmark collection. The website also contains the video of an interview between Maya Angelou and Oprah Winfrey.

Shull, Jodie. *Words of Promise: A Story about James Weldon Johnson.* Minneapolis: Millbrook Press, 2006.

Swain, Gwenyth. *A Hunger for Learning: A Story about Booker T. Washington.* Minneapolis: Millbrook Press, 2006.

Visions: Maya Angelou
http://www.motherjones.com/arts/qa/1995/05/kelley.html
An online version of Ben Kelley's 1995 interview with Maya Angelou. It is part of Mother Jones, an independent nonprofit that publishes *Mother Jones* magazine.

PHOTO ACKNOWLEDGMENTS

The images in this book are used with the permission of: AP/Wide World Photos, pp. 4, 46; Schomburg Center for Research in Black Culture, Marion Post, pp. 7, 8; © Arthur Rothstein/Library of Congress/Hulton Archives, Getty Images, p. 13; Schomburg Center for Research in Black Culture, Russell Lee, pp. 15, 33; © Frederic Lewis/Hulton Archives, Getty Images, p. 19; Schomburg Center for Research in Black Culture, pp. 23 (left), 38; © CORBIS, p. 23 (right); © Bettmann/CORBIS, pp. 35, 47, 73; © The Brett Weston Archive/CORBIS, p. 39; Mary Ellen Mark, p. 56; Library of Congress, pp. 58 (LC-USZC4-1653), 66 (LC-USZ62-117256); © Nik Wheeler/CORBIS, p. 77; © SuperStock, p. 80; Wisconsin Center for Film and Theater Research, pp. 85, 91; © Owen Franken/CORBIS, p. 87; © Will McIntyre/Time & Life Pictures/Getty Images, p. 100; © GARY HENDERSHORN/ Reuters/CORBIS, p. 103.

Front Cover: © Gary Coronado/Palm Beach Post/Zuma Press.